c 2

973
POR

Nevada

Steck-Vaughn Company

Executive Editor	Diane Sharpe
Senior Editor	Martin S. Saiewitz
Design Manager	Pamela Heaney
Photo Editor	Margie Foster
Electronic Cover Graphics	Alan Klemp

Proof Positive/Farrowlyne Associates, Inc.
Program Editorial, Revision Development, Design, and Production

Consultant: Richard Moreno, *Nevada Magazine*

Published by Raintree Steck-Vaughn Publishers, an imprint of Steck-Vaughn Company.

A Turner Educational Services, Inc. book. Based on the Portrait of America television series by R. E. (Ted) Turner.

Cover Photo: Historic Virginia City © by Superstock.

Library of Congress Cataloging-in-Publication Data

Thompson, Kathleen.
    Nevada / Kathleen Thompson.
       p.   cm. — (Portrait of America)
    "Based on the Portrait of America television series"—T.p. verso.
    "A Turner book."
    Includes index.
    ISBN 0-8114-7348-1 (library binding).—ISBN 0-8114-7454-2 (softcover)
    1. Nevada—Juvenile literature. [1. Nevada.] I. Title.
    II. Series: Thompson, Kathleen. Portrait of America.
F841.3.T479 1996
979.3—dc20

                                    95-25730
                                        CIP
                                        AC

Printed and Bound in the United States of America

2 3 4 5 6 7 8 9 10 WZ 03 02 01 00 99

Acknowledgments
The publishers wish to thank the following for permission to reproduce photographs:
P. 7 © Superstock; p. 8 Nevada Historical Society; p. 10 (top) From the Collection of the Lost City Museum/Chester Cobain, (bottom) Nevada Commission on Tourism; pp. 11, 12, 13, 14, 15, 16, 17 Nevada Historical Society; p. 18 U.S. Department of Energy; p. 19 (top) Reuters/Bettmann, (bottom) © Mark Segal/Tony Stone Images; p. 21 (top) Bureau of Reclamation, LC Region Andrew Pernick; p. 22 Nevada Historical Society; p. 23 © Charles Feil/Uniphoto; p. 24 © Uniphoto; p. 26 Nevada Department of Minerals; p. 27 (both) College of Agriculture/University of Nevada; p. 28 Nevada Department of Minerals; p. 29 © Peter Pearson/Tony Stone Images; pp. 30, 31 College of Agriculture/University of Nevada; p. 32 © Steve Vidler/Leo de Wys Inc.; pp. 34, 35, 36 Nevada Commission on Tourism; p. 37 (both) © Kenneth L. Miller; p. 38 Nevada Historical Society; p. 39 MGM Grand Hotel; p. 40 © Tom Campbell/FPG; p. 41 (both) Nevada Commission on Tourism; p. 42 © David Muench/Tony Stone Images; p. 44 © Superstock; p. 46 One Mile Up; p. 47 (left) One Mile Up, (center, right) Nevada Commission on Tourism.

STECK-VAUGHN

PORTRAIT OF AMERICA

Nevada

Kathleen Thompson

A Turner Book

RSVP

RAINTREE
STECK-VAUGHN
PUBLISHERS

The Steck-Vaughn Company

Austin, Texas

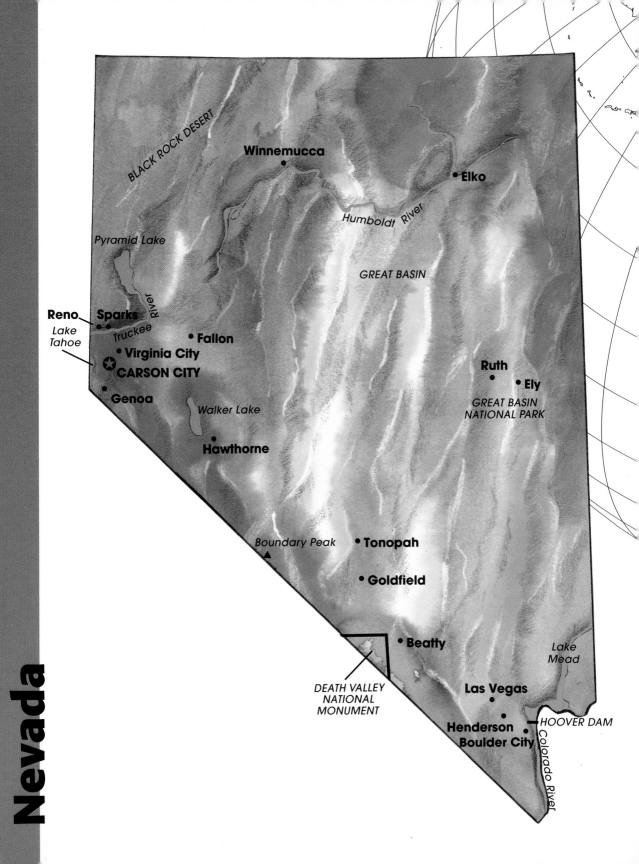

Nevada

BLACK ROCK DESERT

Winnemucca

Elko

Humboldt River

Pyramid Lake

GREAT BASIN

Reno
Sparks
Lake
Tahoe
Truckee River

Fallon

Virginia City
CARSON CITY

Ruth
Ely

GREAT BASIN
NATIONAL PARK

Genoa

Walker Lake

Hawthorne

Boundary Peak
▲

Tonopah

Goldfield

Beatty

Lake
Mead

DEATH VALLEY
NATIONAL
MONUMENT

Las Vegas

Henderson
Boulder City

HOOVER DAM

Colorado River

Contents

Introduction

Nevada is a land of stark beauty and sharp contrasts. It lies within the Great Basin between the Sierra Nevada and the Rocky Mountains. Nevada consists of about 150 mountain ranges, forming a kind of giant washboard of ridges and valleys across the state. Along these slopes grow pine trees up to three thousand years old. Deserts in Nevada are no less beautiful for their columns of giant cactus and twisted rock formations.

Nevada is ancient and modern at the same time. Many Native Americans ranch and farm in the state. Businesses employ thousands of people trained in high-technology careers. Nevadans can divide their time between fast-paced pursuits and a more relaxed way of life. The best of both worlds is available in Nevada.

Nevada's Valley of Fire was named for its red sandstone rocks, not for its temperature, which often reaches more than 100° Fahrenheit.

Nevada

The Hidden Riches

The first people to live in what we now call Nevada arrived about ten thousand years ago. They hunted and gathered seeds and roots. From about A.D. 300 to about 700, a group known as the Basket Makers lived in the area. They were skilled at making water-tight baskets out of reeds and grasses. Unlike the earlier people, this group grew their own food. They also learned to irrigate their crops by directing water to them from rivers through a system of ditches and canals. As their farms grew larger, some groups of the Basket Makers established permanent villages in the southeastern part of the state. They built long, flat houses out of clay. These people came to be known as the Pueblo. Some historians believe that their largest city, Pueblo Grande de Nevada, once had almost twenty thousand inhabitants. The Pueblo civilization disappeared from the Nevada area around 1150.

By the time the first Europeans arrived in the latter part of the eighteenth century, the area was occupied by the Paiute, the Washoe, and the Shoshone. The

Sarah Winnemucca was a Paiute who met with President Rutherford B. Hayes in 1880 to protest the government's mistreatment of the Paiute.

The Pueblo Lost City is a reproduction of a Pueblo town at the Lost City Museum near Overton.

Wind and rain battered the soft clay landscape at Cathedral Gorge for thousands of years, making formations that look like cathedral spires.

Paiute and the Washoe lived in cone-shaped houses made of brush and reeds. The Paiute, who lived near the lakes and wetlands of western Nevada, caught fish and gathered berries, seeds, and roots. The Washoe lived in the same areas and fished and hunted. Each year the Washoe gathered at the shores of Lake Tahoe, a place they considered sacred. The Shoshone lived in the deserts of the Nevada region. They traveled in isolated family groups, returning to certain areas each year to gather plants or hunt small game.

Nevada was one of the last parts of the present-day United States to be explored. One reason was the region's many mountains and deserts. Many historians believe that the Spanish missionary Father Francisco Garcés was the first European to reach present-day Nevada. He traveled up the Colorado River around 1776. From 1826 to 1827, American explorer and trader Jedediah Strong Smith pioneered a route from the Rocky Mountains across what is now central and southern Nevada to the Walker River. British trapper Peter Ogden explored Nevada's Humboldt and Carson rivers in 1828.

In the early 1830s, the federal government sent explorers to map trails across Nevada for settlers traveling to California. The Old Spanish Trail was one of these. This route from Santa Fe to Los Angeles crossed southeastern Nevada. From 1833 to 1834, a group of trappers under army officers Joseph Walker and Benjamin de Bonneville opened a trail that followed the Humboldt River in northern Nevada.

In 1842 John Charles Frémont was sent by the United States government to make maps of the uncharted territory between the Rocky Mountains and California. Around 1843 Frémont reached present-day Nevada. A Paiute chief named Truckee helped lead him across the area between the Rocky Mountains and the Sierra Nevada range. Frémont named this area between the mountains the Great Basin. With Truckee's help, Frémont completed the first map of the Nevada region by 1845.

The United States went to war with Mexico in 1846 because of boundary disputes over western land. Two years later the Treaty of Guadalupe Hidalgo, which ended the Mexican War, transferred most of what is now the western states, including Nevada, to the United States. At that time the region was still mostly uninhabited. Later, in 1848, gold was discovered in the California Territory. Thousands of prospectors journeyed through the Nevada area on their way to California. Not many of them settled there, however.

In 1851 a group of Mormons founded the first permanent settlement

Cooks traveled with most old-time cowboys, bringing wagons such as this one, which were called chuck wagons.

This 1906 photo shows members of the Blue Eagle Ranch. Cattle ranchers first came to Nevada in the 1860s, and sheep ranchers began arriving ten years later.

at Genoa in the Carson River valley. In 1855 Mormons established a mission in the Las Vegas Valley.

In June 1859 prospectors in the Carson River valley uncovered a huge vein of silver called the Comstock Lode. The silver ore was worth $4,791 a ton. Within a month, prospectors from both the West and the East came rushing into Nevada. The town of Virginia City was built on the slopes of what is now Mount Davidson. Smaller towns, such as Silver City and Gold Hill, also sprang up. The population in the Nevada region shot up to almost seven thousand by 1860. In 1861 Congress designated Nevada an official territory.

Native American groups were growing angry at the large number of settlers in the area. The settlers were hunting or scaring away their game and chopping down trees. The situation got worse when some prospectors kidnapped two Paiute women. A group of warriors rescued the women and killed the kidnappers. The Paiute then set up an ambush to attack any of the settlers who might seek revenge. A number of settlers and Paiute were killed in what became known as the Battle of Pyramid Lake. Virginia City residents were furious about the ambush and called on the federal government for help. When army troops arrived, they killed 46 Paiute.

By 1863 Virginia City's population had passed 15,000. This was more than three quarters of the entire Nevada Territory population. Although the population was rising quickly, the territory was still too thinly populated to make it a state. Congress, however, was willing to make an exception for Nevada. The Civil War, which was fought between the Union and the Confederacy, was raging in the East, and the Union needed another state on its side. It also needed the wealth of the Comstock Lode to help finance the war. To get around the issue of the territory's low population, Congress argued that the Comstock Lode would soon bring enough people to the area. Nevada became a state on October 31, 1864. The Union won the Civil War only six months later.

For about ten years, the economy of Nevada boomed. Virginia City came to

Cattle ranchers hired cowboys to look after their herds. This cowboy was employed by the Bell Ranch.

be called the "Queen of the West," known for its ritzy hotels and restaurants. The city also gained a reputation for lawlessness—the town had six churches, but it also had over one hundred saloons!

Silver and gold were being mined throughout central and northern Nevada. In 1869 the Central Pacific Railroad was completed across northern Nevada. The railroad brought more settlers to the state and was used to freight the abundance of gold and silver. By the mid-1870s, the economy of Nevada had become almost entirely dependent on mining. One of Nevada's largest customers was the federal government, which used silver in many of its coins. When the government began replacing silver with a cheaper metal nickel, silver prices decreased. By 1880 the Comstock Lode and the state's smaller mines had begun to run out of silver, and many mines closed.

When the mines closed, thousands of people left Nevada as quickly as they had come. By the mid-1880s, the state's population had dropped by almost a third. Boomtowns became ghost towns in a few short years. The state tried to compensate for the mining losses by encouraging expansion of sheep and cattle ranches. The rich grasses of the mountain valleys in the northern part of the state were especially ideal for ranching, and the industry thrived for a while. Many immigrants, especially people from Spain called Basques, had taken up ranching in the state. But the

This historic photo shows construction workers on the Central Pacific Railroad. The railroad spurred the growth of towns along its path, such as Carlin and Elko.

ranchers ran into problems. As herds expanded good grass became harder to find. In addition the rates ranchers had to pay railroads to ship their cattle were very high. A series of bad winters and hot summers from 1885 to 1887 killed thousands of livestock. Thousands of ranchers went bankrupt and left the state.

For almost forty years, wagon loads of American settlers as well as railroads had pushed their way across the western lands. As a result Native Americans were being forced to live in smaller areas, the buffalo were rapidly being wiped out, and the landscape was changing. In 1888 a Paiute leader named Wovoka had a vision in which the Great Spirit taught him a set of dances called the Ghost Dances. Wovoka's followers believed that performing these dances would bring back the buffalo, cause the settlers to disappear, and reunite all Native Americans, living and dead.

Native Americans throughout the West and the Great Plains soon began performing the Ghost Dances. The federal government quickly outlawed the dances for fear that the dances would lead to more battles. When the Sioux of South Dakota refused to stop, battles did occur. The struggle ended at Wounded Knee Creek, South Dakota, where about 200 Native American men, women, and children were killed.

While Native Americans were being removed from their land and sent to reservations, miners were looking for opportunities to use the land to get rich. More gold and silver deposits were found around the turn of the century, and boomtowns once again sprang

While Paiute leader Wovoka was teaching his followers to perform the Ghost Dances, he also told them to stop fighting and live at peace with the settlers.

up across the state. Copper, first discovered at Ely in 1900, was also a valuable mineral. Copper was used to build and run the nation's factories in the East. More rail lines were built to accommodate the new mines. By 1915 Nevada was crossed by about two thousand miles of track.

When the United States entered World War I in 1917, Nevada was still thriving. Some of the gold and silver mines were beginning to run dry, but industry had made other minerals, such as tungsten and zinc, very valuable. After World War I, however, metal prices fell. Many mines were again forced to shut down, and miners left the state. The population of Goldfield, for example, dropped from twenty thousand to less than two hundred after 1918.

The Great Depression of the 1930s was a time of great economic hardship throughout the United States. Millions of people were unemployed, and banks and factories went out of business. Money was scarce, and prices were very high. In 1931 Nevada became the only state to make gambling legal. It was an attempt to draw more visitors, if not more

This is the Main Street of Palmetto as it appeared in 1906.

In the early 1900s, Dat-so-la-lee gained fame for her traditional Washoe basket weaving. Her baskets had an average of ten stitches per centimeter.

residents, to the state. In 1936 the Hoover Dam, first called the Boulder Dam, was completed. The dam provided hydroelectric, or water-powered, energy. It also provided a new source of irrigation, which spurred a growth in farming.

America's entry into World War II in 1941 brought a brief mining revival in Nevada. Factories in many cities reopened for the purpose of building tanks, airplanes, and boats. When the war ended in 1945, demand fell again. Tourism and the gambling industry compensated the state's economy for the mining and manufacturing losses, however.

Las Vegas opened its first luxury hotel-casino, the Flamingo, in 1946. The state's economy was thriving, but gambling also brought problems to Nevada. The biggest problem was that the gambling casinos attracted criminals. In fact many casinos were run by

This photograph shows the explosion of a 37-kiloton bomb, tested aboveground at the Nevada Test Site on June 24, 1957.

criminals. The state government attached regulations to the gambling industry in the 1950s. A Gaming Control Board was organized by Governor Charles Russell in 1955. The board investigated the background of anyone applying for a casino license.

In 1951 the Atomic Energy Commission exploded an atomic bomb at the Las Vegas Bombing and Gunnery Range for the first time. People for miles around watched the huge explosions, unaware of the harmful effects of the radiation the bombs released. After 1963 such testing was only allowed underground.

The Nevada Test Site is still controversial, however. It is now the largest atomic testing site in the country. People in the area worry that radiation can affect them, even from underground. Many Americans protest nuclear testing at the site. The Nevada government, however, has no desire to shut the site down, because it provides thousands of jobs.

The scarcity of water is another one of Nevada's environmental concerns. The problem was partially resolved in 1963, when the Supreme Court ruled on the use of water from the Colorado River. The Court reassessed the needs of the three states—Arizona, California, and Nevada—that used the river's water and allotted each state a certain amount per year.

Today, Nevada is the fastest-growing state in the nation. Between 1980 and 1990, the number of Nevada residents increased by over fifty percent. In the first half of the 1990s, the population grew by about 25 percent. With the population expanding so rapidly, the state will soon need much more water than the Colorado River can provide. Increased pollution and population congestion are other problems that are unusual for a state that suffered previously from a rising and falling economy and low population. State leaders are considering plans and laws that will give Nevada more power in controlling the impact of its most recent boom.

A protester is dragged away from the Nevada Test Site on March 13, 1994. About 150 protesters held an antinuclear rally outside the site, before entering it to confront military personnel.

Irrigation and air conditioning have made many Nevada communities attractive to retirees.

Hoover Dam

Hoover Dam spans a narrow canyon of the Colorado River on the border between Nevada and Arizona. It's near the place where the river makes a sharp left turn from its western course and plunges south toward the Gulf of California. The dazzle of Las Vegas lies 25 miles to the northwest.

The dam towers 726 feet above the riverbed. Like a giant concrete hand, it blocks the flow of the Colorado River. When Hoover Dam was completed in 1936, it was the largest dam ever built. It's still the highest concrete dam in the Western Hemisphere. In fact there's enough concrete in Hoover Dam to pave a two-lane highway stretching from New York to San Francisco.

That concrete gives the dam the strength to resist the push of the river. At its base, it is 660 feet thick. This base transfers the pressure of the water downward to the solid rock below. The dam's shape helps, too. If you looked at the dam from the top, you would see that it is curved back toward the flow of the river. This arched shape passes the push of the water to the rocky canyon walls.

For thousands of years, people have built dams to control the flow of rivers. Water blocked by a dam piles up behind it to form a lake or reservoir. The purpose is to store extra water that might otherwise flood the land. Water from the reservoir can be used for crop irrigation and other needs during dry times. The dam also lets controlled amounts of water from the lake flow out to keep the river flowing.

Hoover Dam and Lake Mead, the reservoir lying behind it to the north, control the water flow of the Colorado River. This river streams west and south from the Rocky Mountains, carving out the Grand Canyon as it goes. Settlers tried to use its water to irrigate crops, but every spring the river rushed over its banks, destroying property and drowning plants. In late summer it became a trickle, and crops dried up. After a terrible flood ravaged California's Imperial Valley in 1905, people decided the Colorado River had to be tamed. In 1922 the states through which the Colorado and its main branches flowed made an agreement about how to

The power plant at the Hoover Dam is one of the largest hydroelectric plants in the world.

The American Society of Civil Engineers considers the Hoover Dam to be one of the seven modern civil engineering wonders in the United States.

This photo shows construction of the Hoover Dam. When a dam is being built, the water from the river must be diverted while the foundation is put in place.

divide up its water. Once this matter was settled, the United States Congress could authorize a dam. Congress did so in 1928. Construction on the Hoover Dam began in 1931 and lasted five years.

Through the years, Hoover Dam has accomplished what its designers and builders imagined it would. This dam, and others built across the river later, have harnessed the energy of the Colorado to accomplish many things. Lake Mead has made the desert bloom with thriving crops of fruit and vegetables. The lake can irrigate a million acres in Nevada, California, and Arizona.

Thanks to Hoover Dam and others in the system, people in Los Angeles and San Diego can drink pure water from the Colorado River. At Parker Dam, between California and Arizona, water flows into the Colorado River Aqueduct. This series of 29 tunnels carries the water 240 miles to southern California.

Like other modern dams, Hoover Dam produces hydroelectrical power. The river water falling through the dam turns huge turbines. These power the generators that make electricity. This hydroelectric power has advantages. It doesn't harm or use up the water, which just flows on its way after leaving the power plant. It also doesn't pollute the air.

Hoover Dam is one of the nation's largest hydroelectric facilities. In the course of a year, its 17 generators make enough electricity to power half a million homes.

Finally, Hoover Dam has created a recreation area. Throughout the year, Lake Mead and the lands around it attract a steady stream of visitors. They swim, boat, and fish in its waters for bass, trout, and catfish.

In many ways Hoover Dam and others on the Colorado River have made the American Southwest a paradise. Yet problems do exist. By creating lakes and controlling river flow, dams always alter the ecology of their surroundings. There are limits to the amount of water a river can supply.

Today, increasing demands on the Colorado River threaten its existence. Little of its water, for example, now reaches the Gulf of California in Mexico. This has changed the ecology at the mouth of the river for the worse. Species of fish and plants have become extinct. In the twenty-first century, people may need new strategies to reduce the heavy demands on the river.

Lake Mead, the biggest artificially created reservoir in the country, can hold almost two years of flow from the Colorado River. Lake Mead is an ideal place for water-skiing, swimming, fishing, and boating.

An Economy of Pure Gold

The Nevada region was the last place in the United States to be settled by Americans, largely because no one thought the land was worth anything. There wasn't much farmable land—in fact Nevada is still the driest state in the nation. The vast stretches of desert made travel difficult and dangerous. All these factors made Nevada an area where it was hard to live and hard to make a living.

Nevada probably would have waited even longer for settlement if there hadn't been valuable silver and gold under the soil. Today, mining is still an important part of Nevada's economy. A small mining boom in the 1980s nearly doubled the number of miners in the state by the 1990s. In all about 12,500 of Nevada's workers are miners. The state leads the nation in the production of gold, mercury, and magnesite, which is used as an ingredient in making cement, insulation, and rubber. Nevada leads the world in production of turquoise. Silver and oil are also important resources in the state.

Las Vegas is known as the gaming capital of the world. Gambling has created thousands of jobs in Nevada and is one of Nevada's most important tourist attractions.

This huge machine is a drill working in an underground silver mine. Silver is not nearly as important to the state's economy as it was in the late 1800s—gold now earns Nevada more money than silver does.

Agriculture has been an economic activity in Nevada since irrigation systems were built around the 1850s. Irrigation is the method of bringing water from its source to dry lands. Although only about one percent of the state's income comes from agriculture, it's still a way of life for many Nevada residents. Livestock ranching, which has thrived in the state since the 1860s, is Nevada's most important agricultural activity. Almost ninety percent of the state's farmland is devoted to raising cattle, sheep, and horses. An average Nevada ranch is about 3,500 acres, but some are as big as 275,000 acres.

With ranching so important in Nevada, it makes sense that the state's largest crop, alfalfa hay, is grown to feed livestock. Other important crops are barley, wheat, oats, and potatoes. A few Nevada farmers also grow fruits such as grapes, figs, and melons.

The percentage of income brought to the state by farming and mining was long ago overshadowed by tourism. This industry is fueled by the state's thousands of hotels and casinos. Most of the large casinos are in Las Vegas and Reno. Almost 75 percent of the state's population lives and works in those two large cities. More than eighty percent of the people who visit Nevada's casinos are

Cattle ranching is Nevada's most important agricultural activity. Both cattle and sheep ranching take up over fifty million acres of Nevada's land.

Being in the driest state in the nation doesn't stop Nevadans from farming. Irrigation pipes such as these turn desert into lush farmland.

This worker is pouring molten silver and gold from a specialized furnace.

from out of state. Many people also come to Nevada to visit its historic ghost towns, view its natural beauty, and ski on the state's numerous slopes. Nevada's total tourist revenues are about seven billion dollars each year—and the number continues to grow.

Most of Nevada's workers are employed in tourist-related industries. The people who run gaming tables in the casinos, serve visitors at hotels and restaurants, and sell souvenirs at gift shops are all part of a category of jobs called service industries. Service industry workers serve other people instead of manufacture an actual product. Almost ninety percent of Nevada's workers have jobs in some type of service industry.

The most important category of service industries in Nevada is community, social, and personal services. This category includes casino workers, along with lawyers and health care workers. Just over fifty percent of Nevada's service workers fall under this category.

The next most important service industry in Nevada is wholesale and retail trade. Wholesale trade is the buying and selling of large quantities of goods, mostly to businesses. Retail trade is the buying and selling of small quantities of goods, mostly to individual consumers. People who buy a gift, a car, or groceries are participating in retail trade. However, when stores stock up on gifts, cars, or groceries, they usually buy them in large amounts from wholesalers.

In all almost 25 percent of Nevada's service workers fall into the category of wholesale and retail trade.

In addition to creating service jobs, Nevada's casinos indirectly help build up other areas of the state's economy. In fact because gambling brings in about forty percent of the state's income from taxes, the state has recently been able to lower business taxes. As a result hundreds of businesses relocate each year to Nevada to take advantage of its lenient tax laws. Business magazines have singled out Nevada as one of the best places in the nation to run a corporation. This publicity has sparked a population boom in the state. The number of Nevada residents grew by almost 25 percent in the first half of the 1990s, as business owners, workers, and their families moved to Nevada.

Many new businesses in Nevada are involved in manufacturing products. Manufacturing in Nevada brings in about $1.25 billion each year—and that number is growing. Almost thirty thousand Nevadans work in manufacturing. The most important area of manufacturing in Nevada is computers and other electronic equipment. Reno is one of the main areas for this type of manufacturing, although many factories have recently opened up in the Las Vegas area.

Nevada's economy depends largely on tourism and gambling revenues, but the state is working hard to find other ways to create income. It's slow work, but progress is being made, especially in manufacturing. Nevada hopes that in a few more years, people will see it not as a state full of tourists but rather as a model of continuing economic success.

Winter sports are one of Nevada's main tourist draws. This photo shows skiers in the Las Vegas region, but most of Nevada's winter sports enthusiasts visit the area around Reno and Lake Tahoe.

The Loneliest Job in Nevada

Ranching can be a very lonely profession. A rancher has to get used to spending long periods of time with only a horse, a couple of dogs, and a herd of sheep or cattle for company.

Some people, however, thrive on this lonely lifestyle. Cattle rancher Ted Zimmerman is one of these people. "It's not hard," said Ted. "It's not grueling to me to get up in the morning and go out. But there's always one thing—if you get tired and whatever, you can lay down and go to sleep anyplace because you're the boss. I enjoy this type of work. It's not the same thing day in and day out. So I always look forward to going to work. . . . People ask me, 'When are you going to take a vacation?' And I tell them, 'I'm on vacation every day.'"

It wasn't that easy for Ted's wife, Julie, to get used to the ranching

Sheepherders often have to spend weeks at a time in the desert watching their sheep. However, for now, this herd of sheep is home at the S Bar S Ranch.

Livestock is raised on almost 90 percent of Nevada's farmland.

lifestyle. "It probably took me about seven years to adjust to ranch life, to get to the point where I think now I would like to stay here," Julie remembered. "Seven years ago I would have given anything, almost, to go back to the city. And I used to long to go and visit with people and talk to people, and I still do, but not as much as I used to. And I have gotten used to the solitude out here. . . . [B]ut the only reason I stayed was because I love Ted."

Fourteen-year-old Jed Hedges, born into a ranching family near Elko, plans to spend his life tending cattle. Jed plans on studying ranch manage-ment in college, then returning to Nevada to run his own small herd after he graduates. Jed and his family are more than thirty miles away from their closest neighbor. They are nowhere near a public school, so Jed takes correspondence courses. These are courses that are completed at home by receiving and sending materials through the mail.

The life of a rancher is a lifestyle that has been crucial to Nevada's econ-omy for over a century, but it's not for everyone. However, for people who enjoy working alone without feeling lonely, there's no better profession around.

Gifts from the Past

Some people consider Las Vegas, with its bright lights and gambling casinos, an example of a culture that is uniquely American. The world's most famous performers—from top rock bands to Russia's Bolshoi Ballet—almost always make a stop in Las Vegas when they're on tour. Las Vegas is not the only sign of culture there is in the state, however. Although the cultural contributions of Native Americans, Basques, and early settlers are not amplified or brightly lit, they have lasted much longer.

The oldest culture of Nevada is that of the Native Americans. Powwows, festivals, and rodeos are held throughout the year by Paiute, Washoe, and Shoshone groups. Dancing is the most spectacular aspect of these gatherings, and both the costume styles and the dances have been passed down through the centuries.

Methods of creating handcrafted jewelry, baskets, and textiles have been preserved and followed by Nevada's Native Americans. The Washoe have gained fame for their skill in basketry, largely thanks to the

Virginia City was once one of the richest places in the world. In the 1800s it produced a billion dollars worth of silver and gold. Today, Virginia City is maintained as a historical frontier town.

work of Dat-so-la-lee, a basket maker in the early 1900s. Her baskets were so unique and well made that word of her skill eventually spread across the nation. By the time Dat-so-la-lee died in 1925, some of her baskets sold for as much as three thousand dollars. The Nevada State Museum in Carson City and the Nevada Historical Society in Reno both hold large collections of the baskets of this talented Washoe artist.

The Basques came to Nevada from Spain in the 1880s as sheepherders. They have maintained their traditions through their annual festivals and strong ethnic ties. The largest festival, the National Basque Festival, is held in Elko each July. Basques in colorful traditional dress celebrate by dancing, singing, and cooking. Many festivals include demonstrations of Basque skills such as herding.

Elko is also the host for the yearly Cowboy Poetry Gathering. Cowboys in the Old West used to be alone on the trail for days, and many of them passed the time by making up rhymed stories. When they met other cowboys at campsites along the trail, they often shared these stories. This tradition has been preserved by Elko's Cowboy Poetry Gathering, held every January.

Downtown Las Vegas is the best-known part of Nevada's culture.

Mining towns that grew up in the early silver and gold rush days are another part of Nevada's culture. Boomtowns, such as Goldfield and Silver City, used to boast as many as twenty thousand residents. Now only a few hundred live in either town. Some old mining towns in the state are abandoned completely. All of these towns carry the spirit of the Wild West, and many original and restored buildings help us imagine what life there was like.

The Wild West is also remembered in the novels of Nevada writer Walter Van Tilburg Clark. His 1945 book, *City of Trembling Leaves*, is based in Reno, where he spent his youth. Clark's most famous book is *The Ox-Bow Incident*, first published in 1940 and made into a film only three years later. Nevada is also the subject of most of Clark's works of nonfiction.

Samuel Clemens is best-known for his books *The Adventures of Tom Sawyer* and *Adventures of Huckleberry Finn*. Clemens began writing under the name Mark Twain for the first time as a columnist for Virginia City's newspaper *Territorial Enterprise*. His travel book *Roughing It* includes an account of time he spent in Nevada in the early 1860s.

Nevada's culture is made possible by the respect Nevadans have for great things that have come before. That is why it has carried on, and that is also why it will continue to grow.

This traditional Native American dancer is competing at the Fallon Powwow, which is held every May.

Preserving a Way of Life

The Paiute have lived around Pyramid Lake in northwestern Nevada for centuries. They have depended on the fish of the lake—the cutthroat trout and the rare cui-ui—for just as long. The Paiute are proud descendants of the Kuyuidokado, who lived by Pyramid Lake even before the Europeans arrived. *Paiute* means "cui-ui eaters."

Beulah Fajardo, a Pyramid Lake Paiute, relates many stories about her ancestors. "They believed in things," she said. "They always said that if you have good words for the lake, the lake will be good to you. As long as they could remember, they had been around the lake. . . . And they never had a bad word for the lake. It's something, I guess, that they had seen so many years that they just grew to love it."

Pyramid Lake and the Paiute Reservation are part of the immense, dry expanse of the Great Basin. This region stretches between the Rocky Mountains and the Sierra Nevadas. One reason why Fajardo's Kuyuidokado ancestors developed such a respect for the lake is that they needed its water to survive. The Kuyuidokado depended on the lake, in a very real sense, for their life.

Beulah Fajardo and the Paiute continue to look to Pyramid Lake for survival. However, there was a time when they feared that the lake would no longer be able to support them. In

This distinctive rock formation inspired army officer and explorer John C. Frémont to name the area Pyramid Lake in 1844.

Technicians at the hatchery study Pyramid Lake's fish carefully and keep detailed logs on their development.

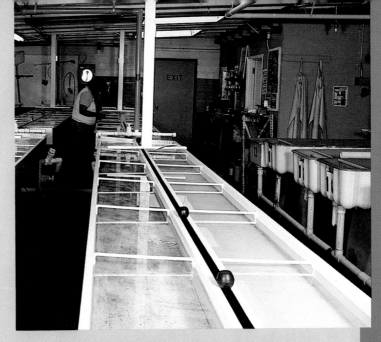

Small fish are raised in these trays at Pyramid Lake's hatchery, then released into the lake to keep the fish population from declining.

the late 1800s, settlers and miners built towns south of Lake Pyramid. They constructed a dam on the Truckee River, which feeds the lake, to redirect water to their settlements. As a result Pyramid Lake's water level sank lower, and the fish began to die off.

Beginning in the 1970s, the Paiute began restoring the fish in Pyramid Lake. They built a hatchery to breed other kinds of fish. They also worked closely with the United States Fish and Wildlife Service to study how the fish adapted to the lake's changing environment. Their

efforts have been a success. Pyramid Lake's fish population has increased in number and size. Today, the Paiute's work is admired and studied by lake preservationists worldwide.

Beulah Fajardo and the Paiute never lost faith in their lake. "Looking back," said Fajardo, "the lake has always provided for the people, and I think the future of the lake is going to be the same." The Pyramid Lake Paiute have discovered that technology, when it's used in the right spirit, can work with the old way of life.

37

Viva Las Vegas

Although gambling wasn't legalized in Nevada until 1931, the state was full of gamblers of a different sort long before then. Nevada's silver and gold prospectors came to Nevada by the thousands, lured by stories of people striking it rich. Las Vegas casino owner Jack Binion still tells one of these stories.

"In the 1870s," said Binion, "the Paiute occupied this area, and up on the top of Kokoweefe Peak they discovered a cavern and worked their way down to the bottom of the cavern. And in the bottom they found . . . an incredible amount of gold. But while they were working this gold out, one of the Paiute boys was killed. And they made a law that they could never return to the caverns again. So they blocked it up, and people have been looking for it ever since."

Most of Nevada's prospectors are long gone. But stories of striking it rich live on—although they no longer involve picks and shovels and nuggets of silver and gold. Binion tells one of these stories about his casino, the Horseshoe. "We let a guy bet $777,000 one time, probably the largest bet that's ever been made in a gambling house," said Binion. "He showed up here one afternoon—kind of late in the afternoon—with two little suitcases, one full of money and one empty, for the money he was going to win. He was optimistic, I'll say that. We converted his money to chips and he bet it . . . and he won." The man became a legend in an instant, doubling his $777,000 and walking out with his second suitcase full, just as he had planned.

This photo shows Las Vegas in 1906. The town was so small at that time that it had to call itself the "Gateway to Goldfield" to get any attention.

The MGM Grand Casino is the world's largest hotel, casino, and theme park. If one person wanted to spend one night in every room in the hotel, it would take almost 14 years.

Stories like Binion's have kept people coming to Las Vegas for almost 75 years now. In the first half of the 1990s, about 25 million visitors came each year, hoping to become the next legendary big winner. But as gambling is being legalized in more and more states, especially on riverboats, Las Vegas casino owners are realizing that they have to make their style of gambling unique to keep people coming. Many of them have gone far beyond unique—these days some of the casinos are downright outrageous.

Take the one-billion-dollar MGM Grand hotel-casino. The entrance is spectacular enough in itself—visitors walk between the front paws of a gigantic golden lion to enter the main doors. But the lion wasn't enough for MGM—it spent hundreds of millions more dollars to build a 33-acre

Roulette is one of the most popular games at Las Vegas casinos.

amusement park next door. For a different kind of spectacle, the Mirage casino has turned itself into a casino-zoo, with real dolphins and rare white tigers. Perhaps the most amazing show is at the Treasure Island, where pirate ships battle in front of the casino every hour and a half. These battles are fought to the finish, with explosions and the losing ship actually being sunk!

Identical models of famous and historical sites are also popular casino themes. The Luxor borrows from ancient Egypt, complete with huge pyramids and a sphinx. The New York New York Casino is a model of Manhattan in New York City—not just the Empire State Building and the World Trade Center, but *all* of Manhattan's famous landmarks. The Dunes Casino has been replaced by the Bellagio resort casino complete with a 12-acre lake.

Some people come to Las Vegas for other reasons than to gamble. They also come to get married! About 150,000 people a year marry in Las Vegas, and most of them come from out of state. Like Las Vegas itself, the weddings specialize in having fun. For example, at the Graceland Chapel, couples are married by an Elvis Presley impersonator. And after the ceremony, what better place to spend a honeymoon than Las Vegas? There is entertainment 24 hours a day, fun, food, and famous stars.

No matter how much glitz and glitter Las Vegas has, however, the main attraction will always be the same. It's the opportunity for each and every visitor to become the next big winner—the next lucky person the locals will talk about for years to come. That story, forever told and retold, is both the history and the future of this glittering desert oasis.

Casinos in Clark County, where Las Vegas is located, generate about four hundred million dollars in winnings each month.

Hundreds of extravagant shows are staged in Las Vegas every day.

A Safe Bet for the Future

Not too long ago, Nevada's economy was almost entirely dependent on its income from tourists and gambling. This was dangerous, because if tourism dropped in Nevada, its economy would be severely affected.

In the past decade, however, Nevada has taken steps to make its financial future more secure. Nevada's main focus has been to attract new or relocated businesses. By the 1990s Nevada's efforts had brought a measure of success. Nevada was the only state in the nation that reported manufacturing job growth in the first half of the 1990s. It also consistently ranks in the top ten nationally for overall job growth. In addition Nevada's population is growing along with the businesses. Nevada was the fastest-growing state in the nation in the first half of the 1990s.

All these achievements have uncovered a few problems still waiting for solutions. The percentage of Nevadans living below the poverty level increased in the first half of the 1990s. The number rose from 10.2

Great Basin National Park preserves Nevada's unique desert environment for future generations. Great Basin was Nevada's first national park.

Reno calls itself "The Biggest Little City in the World" because it mixes small-town friendliness with the convenience of a big city.

percent to about 11.1 percent. In addition increased population and industry have caused increased pollution of Nevada's air and water.

Another problem accompanying Nevada's population growth is its dwindling water supply. The state's average 7.5 inches of rain and snow each year do not provide nearly enough water. Nevada has created reservoirs, such as Lake Mead, and drawn water from underground reservoirs. But these water sources, especially those underground, are diminishing as more and more people and industries use them. Possible solutions to this problem include finding new water sources or restricting water use across the state.

Nevada is not gambling its natural resources against the future. There are creative ways to guard against ruining the environment while continuing to grow. Nevada has the chance to be the forerunner in finding a solution everyone can live with.

Important Historical Events

1150 The Pueblo civilization disappears from Nevada.

1776 The first European explorer to pass through the area is probably the Spanish missionary Father Francisco Garcés.

1826 to 1827 American explorer Jedediah Strong Smith pioneers a route through what is now central and southern Nevada.

1828 British trapper Peter Ogden explores Nevada's Humboldt and Carson rivers.

1830 The Old Spanish Trail cuts across Nevada to make way for California settlers.

1833 to 1834 Joseph Walker and Benjamin de Bonneville lead an expedition along the Humboldt River.

1843 to 1845 John C. Frémont explores the Great Basin and completes the first map of the area.

1848 The Treaty of Guadalupe Hidalgo gives the United States the Nevada region, along with California, Utah, and parts of four other present-day states.

1851 A group of Mormons found Nevada's first permanent settlement.

1859 The Comstock Lode is discovered at present-day Virginia City.

1861 The Nevada Territory is created by Congress in March. The Civil War begins in the East in April.

1864 Nevada is made the thirty-sixth state.

1869 The first transcontinental railroad is completed across northern Nevada.

1888 Paiute leader Wovoka begins to teach the Ghost Dances to Native Americans across the country.

1900 Huge deposits of silver are discovered. Copper is discovered in the state for the first time at Ely.

1917 World War I gives a boost to Nevada's mining industry.

1918 Nevada's economy plummets again with the end of World War I.

1931 Nevada becomes the only state with legalized gambling.

1939 World War II creates new business for Nevada mines.

1945 Demand for Nevada's mining falls again with the end of World War II.

1946 The Flamingo, Las Vegas's first luxury hotel-casino, opens.

1951 The United States begins a series of nuclear weapons tests in Nevada.

1955 Governor Charles Russell establishes a state Gaming Control Board.

1963 Nevada moves its nuclear testing underground to comply with the Nuclear Test-Ban Treaty. The United States Supreme Court sets limits on the amount of water Arizona, California, and Nevada may take from the Colorado River each year.

1970 The Pyramid Lake Paiute begin restoring and preserving the lake's fish.

1986 Nevada opens its first national park, Great Basin National Park.

1992 A six-year drought ends.

1995 Nevada ranks as the fastest-growing state in the nation for the first half of the decade.

Nevada's flag is yellow, green, and white on a blue background. Above a white star and the state name is a yellow banner with the phrase "Battle Born," referring to Nevada's acceptance into the Union in the midst of the Civil War. The wreath below the star is made of two sprigs of sagebrush, Nevada's state flower.

Nevada Almanac

Nickname. The Silver State

Capital. Carson City

State Bird. Mountain bluebird

State Flower. Sagebrush

State Tree. Bristlecone pine and single-leaf piñon

State Motto. All for Our Country

State Song. "Home Means Nevada"

State Abbreviations. Nev. (traditional); NV (postal)

Statehood. October 31, 1864, the 36th state

Government. Congress: U.S. senators, 2; U.S. representatives, 2. State Legislature: senators, 21; representatives, 42. Counties: 16, plus independent Carson City

Area. 110,567 sq mi (286,367 sq km), 7th in size among the states

Greatest Distances. north/south, 478 mi (770 km); east/west, 318 mi (511 km)

Elevation. Highest: Boundary Peak, 13,140 ft (4,005 m). Lowest: 470 ft (143 m)

Population. 1990 Census: 1,206,152 (50.1% increase over 1980), 39th among the states. Density: 11 persons per sq mi (4 persons per sq km). Distribution: 85% urban, 15% rural. 1980 Census: 800,493

Economy. Agriculture: Beef cattle, sheep, horses, alfalfa hay, barley, wheat, oats, potatoes, grapes, figs, melons. Manufacturing: electronic equipment, printed materials. Mining: gold, silver, oil, magnesite, mercury, turquoise, copper

State Seal

State Flower: Sagebrush

State Bird: Mountain bluebird

Annual Events

★ Cowboy Poetry Gathering in Elko (January)

★ Boulder City Spring Jamboree (April)

★ Helldorado Days in Las Vegas (May)

★ Desert Oasis Bluegrass Festival in Fallon (June)

★ Reno Rodeo (June)

★ All-Indian Rodeo and Stampede Indian Days Powwow in Fallon (July)

★ National Basque Festival in Elko (July)

★ Nevada State Fair in Reno (August)

★ Pony Express Days in Ely (August)

★ National Championship Air Races in Reno (September)

★ Pyramid Lake Rodeo in Nixon (September)

Places to Visit

★ Death Valley National Park, near Beatty

★ Fleischmann Planetarium, at the University of Nevada in Reno

★ Great Basin National Park, near Baker

★ Hoover Dam, near Las Vegas

★ Lake Tahoe

★ Las Vegas Strip

★ Lost City Museum, near Overton

★ Nevada State Museums in Carson City and Las Vegas

★ Pyramid Lake, near Reno

★ Valley of Fire in Clark County

★ Virginia and Truckee Railroad in Virginia City

★ Wild Horse State Recreation Area north of Elko